Most-Used Words and Phrases

series 90

John Robert Gregg
Louis A. Leslie
Charles E. Zoubek
Shorthand written by Jerome P. Edelman

McGraw-Hill Book Company
New York · St. Louis · Dallas · San Francisco
Auckland · Bogotá · Düsseldorf · Johannesburg · London
Madrid · Mexico · Montreal · New Delhi · Panama · Paris
São Paulo · Singapore · Sydney · Tokyo · Toronto

Gregg Shorthand Most-Used Words and Phrases, Series 90
Copyright © 1978, 1963 by McGraw-Hill, Inc. All Rights Reserved.
Copyright 1949 by McGraw-Hill Book Company, Inc. All Rights
Reserved. Copyright renewed 1977. No part of this publication may
be reproduced, stored in a retrieval system, or transmitted, in any
form or by any means, electronic, mechanical, photocopying, re-
cording, or otherwise, without the prior written permission of the
publisher.

2 3 4 5 6 7 8 9 FGRFGR 8 7 6 5 4

First McGraw Hill Trade Edition, 1984

ISBN 0-07-024487-1

Library of Congress Cataloging in Publication Data

Gregg, John Robert, date.
    Most-used words and phrases, series 90.
    Includes index.
    1. Shorthand—Gregg—Dictionaries. I. Leslie,
Louis A., date   joint author. II. Zoubek, Charles E.,
date   joint author. III. Title.
Z55.5.G76 1978   653'.427'03   77-867

ISBN 0-07-024487-1

Preface

Gregg Shorthand, Most-Used Words and Phrases, Series 90, is a compilation of 3,981 words and 1,404 phrases classified according to the lessons of *Gregg Shorthand, Series 90*. Each word and phrase, together with its shorthand outline, is listed in the lesson and with the principle of *Gregg Shorthand, Series 90*, under which it can first be written.

Selection of Words

The words in this list were selected after a careful analysis of four studies of words frequently used in business and one study of words frequently used in general communication.

The words that appear in this list are those that, in the opinion of the authors, are of the greatest usefulness to the stenographer in the business office.

Many of the words that appear in the five frequency lists analyzed by the authors are simple derivatives using -*ing*, -*s*, and -*ed*, derivatives that the shorthand writer can build without any difficulty from the primitive forms. Consequently, only a few of these derivatives have been included. However, derivatives that present some stenographic problems are given. Thus the 3,981 words in *Gregg Shorthand, Most-Used Words and Phrases, Series 90*, actually represent a considerably larger vocabulary.

Selection of Phrases

The selection of the shorthand phrases in *Gregg Shorthand, Most-Used Words and Phrases, Series 90*, is based largely on the business-letter phrase-frequency study in which the authors analyzed the phrase content of 2,500 business letters containing more than 250,000 running words. In this study the authors found 3,536 different phrases, of which 1,404 are given in this book.

Each phrase, with its shorthand outline, is given in the lesson in which it can first be written.

Distribution of Words and Phrases

As a result of the elimination of a few word-building principles, brief forms, and word beginnings and endings, as well as the rearrangement of the order of presentation of brief forms in *Gregg Shorthand,*

Series 90, many useful business words and phrases can now be written in the early lessons.

For example, *w* is now presented in Lesson 4; consequently, words like *we, way,* and *week,* and phrases like *we are* and *we will* are available in Lesson 4 instead of in Lesson 13 as in *Gregg Shorthand, Diamond Jubilee Series.* Words like *invite, inside,* and *indeed* are available in Lesson 3 instead of in Lesson 26 as in *Gregg Shorthand, Diamond Jubilee Series.*

The early availability of these frequently used words and phrases makes possible the construction of smooth, natural business practice material almost from Lesson 1.

Distribution of Words and Phrases

Chapter	Words	Phrases
1	968	377
2	734	536
3	527	182
4	589	100
5	430	81
6	300	108
7	275	9
8	158	11
TOTALS	3,981	1,404

500 Frequently Used Words

A feature that teachers will find helpful is the list of 500 of the most frequently used words in the English language presented in alphabetical order. This list appears in the appendix.

Index

In the back of *Gregg Shorthand, Most-Used Words and Phrases, Series 90,* is an alphabetical index of all the words included in the book, together with an indication of the lesson in which they appear.

It is the hope of the authors that teachers will find the lists in this book useful in their shorthand teaching.

Louis A. Leslie
Charles E. Zoubek

chapter 1
lesson 1

- **S-Z, A, F, V**

face	safe	say
phase	save	vase

- **E**

cease	fee	see
ease	fees	sees
easy	sea	

- **N**

knee	sane	seen
navy	scene	vain

- **M**

aim	may	name
fame	me	same
main	mean	seem

- **T**

ate	meat	stay
east	neat	steam
faced	safety	tame
fate	seat	tea
feet	stain	team

▪ D

aid		deed		need	
date		feed		saved	
day		made		stayed	

lesson 2

▪ O

dome		note		stone	
foam		own		stove	
foe		phone		stow	
know		sew		tone	
known		snow		vote	
no		so		zone	

▪ R

dear		heir		read	
door		more		remade	
drain		near		remain	
drove		nor		remote	
fair		or		rename	
fare		radio		road	
free		rain		stereo	
freight		rate		store	

storm	tore	treat
story	torn	treaty
stream	trade	wrote

▪ L

deal	lead	railroad
fail	leave	real
feel	loan	really
floor	low	relief
flow	mail	relieve
lady	meal	retail
late	rail	roll

▪ H

hair	heat	hole
haste	heed	home
he	heel	whole
hear	here	wholly

▪ WORD ENDING -ING

| aiming | heating | mailing |
| hearing | lading | rating |

▪ Ī

airline	fight	height
drive	file	hide
dry	flight	hire
dye	fly	iron

life	my	smile
light	night	strive
line	rely	style
lining	right	tire
might	side	title
mile	sight	tried
mine	sign	write

▪ OMISSION OF MINOR VOWELS

dealer	leader	oral
driver	lower	owner
easiest	meter	reader
Easter	minor	rider
even	motive	roller
evening	motor	season
favor	native	total
final	normal	totally
hasten	normally	trailer
heater	notify	vital
later	nylon	writer

lesson 3

▪ BRIEF FORMS

a .   am ____   an .

are ⌣	I ⌀	not —
at ⟋	in —	our ⌣
have ⟩	it ⟋	well ⌣
hour ⌣	Mr. ⌒	will ⌣

▪ WORD BEGINNING IN-

indeed	inside	invite

▪ PHRASES

Have

have made	I have made	it will have
have not	I have not	may have
he may have	I have tried	might have
he will have	I may have	will have
I have	I will have	will not have

I

I am	I mean	I say
I drove	I might	I see
I fear	I need	I will
I feel	I need not	I will not
I know	I remain	I wrote

Will, Well

he will	I will	well known
he will not	I will not	will not

Miscellaneous

in it	in our	it will

it will not · may not · might not

■ LEFT S-Z

days	lines	seats
frames	means	seems
frozen	most	series
highest	names	sides
homes	needs	slice
hours	niece	slide
ice	race	slight
its	raise	source
knows	realize	styles
ladies	release	wholesale
lease	rise	wills
least	rose	writers
license	sales	zeal

■ P

deep	peace	pleased
hope	people	pole
open	piece	police
paid	pipes	post
pair	place	postal
paper	plain	postdate
pay	plate	postpaid
payroll	please	postpone

postpones   prize   spare

praise   proceed   speed

precede   promote   supplied

premium   propose   suppose

prepaid   proposed   supposed

prepare   provide   supreme

price   ropes   tape

primary   soap   type

private   space   typewriter

▪ B

able   born   fiber

base   brief   label

bear   bright   labor

blame   buy   library

bolt   buyer   neighbors

▪ PHRASES

at least   I realize   in its

he knows   I suppose   will pay

he needs   I will see   will see

lesson 4

▪ OO

blue   do   drew

due	new	roof
during	news	room
duty	noon	route
fireproof	pool	routine
food	poor	rule
fruit	presume	suit
hereto	produce	to
influence	producers	too
knew	proof	tool
lieu	prove	tour
loose	prune	true
lose	reduce	two
move	removal	who
movers	renew	whom
neutral	renewal	whose

■ W, SW, WH

highway	wave	wheat
likewise	way	wheel
sweet	we	while
swear	wear	white
waist	weigh	why
wait	weighed	wide
waiver	weight	wife
waste	whale	wire

wise   wives   woven

■ K

acre	course	locate
basic	courtesy	make
bouquet	cream	maker
break	crew	reclaim
broke	cried	recline
broker	crude	recruit
cake	cry	remake
came	cycle	retake
care	declare	sake
career	decline	scale
case	decrease	scheme
claim	include	school
clean	inclusive	scope
clear	increase	score
clearer	instruct	screen
close	instructive	skiing
coal	instructor	smoke
coast	keep	specific
cool	keys	spoke
corn	lake	strike
corner	like	take
coupon	locally	taken

vacancies	weak	week

▪ G (GAY)

degree	glued	grew
eager	go	gross
gain	goal	group
gale	goes	grouped
game	grade	grow
gate	grain	grown
gates	gray	guide
gave	great	legal
gear	greater	legally
girls	green	organ
gleam	greeting	regain

▪ PHRASES

Do

do it	do so	I do not say
do not	I do	I do not see
do not have	I do not	

To

to care	to close	to its
to claim	to gain	to keep
to clean	to go	to take
to clear	to grow	to taste
to climb	to it	to tie

11
LESSON 4

to train ⟋ to try ⟋ to whom ⟋

We

we are — we have not — we might not
we are not — we knew — we need
we do — we know — we note
we do not — we made — we take
we do not say — we make — we try
we do not see — we may — we will
we feel — we may have — we will have
we have — we mean — we will not
we have made — we might — we will see

Who

who are — who knows — who may
who do not — who made — who might
who have — who make — who might have
who have made — who makes — who will

Miscellaneous

gave me — he knew — I like
he came — I came — I make
he gave — I gave — in case
he liked — I knew — in lieu

lesson 5

▪ A

absence	appeal	bad
absolute	appear	bag
accrued	appearance	balance
accuracy	apply	barrel
accurate	appraisal	battery
act	approval	black
active	approve	campaign
activity	approved	capacity
add	arrears	capital
adhere	arrival	carrier
advance	arrive	carry
advice	arrives	cast
again	as	category
against	aside	class
aggregate	ask	classified
ago	assume	data
agree	astray	draft
alone	attractive	drag
amazing	avenue	fabric
ample	back	fact
apiece	backed	factor

12

factory	lapse	sacrifice
fast	last	sad
flag	lasts	salary
flat	magazine	salesman
gas	man	sample
gasoline	map	scatter
glance	married	scrap
glass	master	sedan
graphic	material	slack
graphs	matters	staff
grass	narrower	stamp
gratified	pack	swam
gratifying	pads	tags
habit	panel	tariff
had	pass	task
half	passed	track
happen	past	traffic
happy	plan	traveler
has	postmaster	varied
hats	proposal	vary
laboratory	ran	vast
lack	rapid	wagon
lamps	ratify	wrap

■ Ä

alarm	cargo	mark
arm	carload	marked
army	dark	park
art	far	postmark
bargain	farm	smart
car	harm	star
carbon	heart	start

■ E

accept	closest	felt
address	currency	finest
addressed	desk	get
assets	effect	greatest
basket	effective	guess
bed	elect	happiness
beg	else	harvest
begged	enable	head
belt	enact	heavy
best	enamel	help
better	error	helpless
bread	favorite	homeless
breakfast	federal	hotel
cabinet	fell	invest
cancel	fellow	kept

latest	negative	seller
leaflet	net	sells
led	newest	semester
left	orchestra	senate
leg	pamphlet	senator
less	parcel	sense
lessons	poems	separate
let	poetry	set
letter	poets	settle
letterhead	presence	slowest
letters	professor	specify
level	protect	spread
lowest	protest	step
market	ready	sweater
mechanism	regret	swell
medal	relative	technique
medicine	remedy	telephone
member	remember	tell
memory	rest	test
met	said	testify
metal	secret	verified
motel	secretarial	verify
nearest	secretary	veteran
needless	select	west

wet · · · · wetness · · ·

■ l

admit	did	illness
arisen	dig	inactive
artist	dramatic	investigate
been	drastic	kill
benefit	drill	kit
bid	duplicate	liberal
bidding	elastic	liberty
bids	facilitate	limit
big	familiar	list
bigger	fill	listen
biggest	film	little
bigness	finance	live
billing	fiscal	merit
bills	gift	middle
built	give	military
busy	given	milk
chemistry	guilty	mill
Christmas	him	miss
cigars	history	notice
city	hit	omit
civic	if	pencil
dictate	ignore	pick

pin	ribbon	still
plastic	risk	swivel
postscript	river	territory
practice	sanitary	tickets
predict	sickness	trip
prettiest	silver	typist
pretty	similar	vicinity
principal	simple	victory
principally	since	visit
prohibit	sincere	win
remit	solicit	witness

■ OBSCURE VOWEL

answer	fur	service
certificate	grocery	surface
certified	her	surprise
circle	hurry	survey
clerk	hurt	tracer
earn	infer	urban
earnest	insert	versatile
energy	learn	worries
firm	prefer	worse
first	serve	worst

■ OVER TH

bath	booth	death

faith	theft	thickness
method	theme	thief
smooth	then	thin
sympathize	these	tooth
teeth	thick	truth
theater	thicker	width

▪ UNDER TH

birth	healthy	three
birthday	lathe	thrill
both	north	throat
clothing	thorough	through
earth	those	throw
growth	though	thrown
health	thread	wealth

▪ PHRASES

as if	as well	has made
as it	at last	has met
as it will	at these	has no
as these	did not	has not
as though	give me	have had
as to	had not	he did
as we	has given	he did not
as we are	has had	he fell
as we have	has known	he felt

he gets

he left

he lives

he said

I did

I did not

I felt

I get

I give

I guess

I have had

I left

I live

I met

I notice

I ran

I read

I said

if it

if my

if so

if these

if we

if we do

if we have

in fact

in these

it has

since then

these are

through its

through these

to cancel

to carry

to get

to give

to tell

to these

to travel

we did

we did not

we get

we give

we have given

we have had

we have not had

we notice

who have had

■ BRIEF FORMS

but

can

cannot

can't

his

is

Mrs.

of

that

the

with

withdrew

you

your

yours

▪ PHRASES

Can

can have	I can see	we cannot
he can	if we can	we can say
he can make	if we cannot	we can't
he can't	we can	who can
I can	we can have	who can say
I cannot	we can make	who cannot

Is, His

as it is	if it is	is the
he is	in his	it is
he is not	is it	to his
here is	is not	who is

Of

of his	of its	of the
of it	of our	of these

That

as that	in that	that are
as to that	is that	that are not
ask that	is that the	that do not
at that	of that	that have
hope that	realize that	that is
hope that the	so that	that is not
if that is	so that the	that is the

that it has

that our

that will not

that it is

that the

through that

that it will

that these

to that

that may

that will

with that

The

as the

has the

make the

as to the

if the

realize the

ask the

in the

through the

at the

in the last

to the

With

with him

with our

with the

You

as you

ask you

if you cannot

as you are

asking you

if you did not

as you can

can you

if you do

as you did

do you

if you do not

as you go

give you

if you get

as you have

giving you

if you go

as you know

have you

if you have

as you may

hope you will

if you have not

as you may have

if you

if you know

as you say

if you are

if you let

as you will

if you are not

if you need

as you will see

if you can

if you see

if you will

if you will have

if you will see

of you

serving you

to you

with you

you are

you are not

you can

you can have

you can see

you cannot

you cannot see

you can't

you did

you did not

you do

you do not

you have

you have had

you have made

you have not

you have seen

you know

you made

you make

you may

you may have

you may not

you might

you might have

you might not

you need

you need not

you say

you see

you will

you will have

you will not

you will not have

you will see

Your

as to your

as your

ask your

have your

if your

of your

of yours

to your

with your

your name

your needs

your note

chapter 2
lesson 7

■ SH

assurance	machine	shelf
assure	machinery	shell
assures	measure	shelves
brochure	pleasure	ship
cash	pressure	shipped
cashier	ratio	shoe
casually	sash	shoes
dishes	shade	shoot
finish	shall	show
fresh	shape	shown
garage	shaped	shows
hosiery	shapes	sure
insurance	share	treasure
insure	sharp	treasurer
issue	she	treasury
issues	sheets	visual

■ CH

achieve	approached	catch
approach	branch	chain

chains	chest	match
chair	chickens	porch
chairman	chief	ranch
chance	choose	reach
chapter	chose	rich
chart	chosen	search
cheap	church	sketch
cheaper	each	speech
cheapest	franchise	switch
check	inch	teacher
cheese	kitchen	torch

■ J

age	charged	jelly
agencies	cordial	jewel
agency	courage	jewelers
aging	edges	jewelry
arrange	generate	journal
average	hinges	juries
baggage	imagine	jury
bridge	injure	juvenile
brokerage	injury	large
challenge	jail	larger
change	jam	largest
charge	jar	ledger

major	originally	range
margin	package	siege
merge	page	storage
messages	passenger	strategy
mortgage	pledge	surgeon
oblige	postage	urge
original	rage	wages

■ O

adopt	copier	honest
block	copies	honesty
blotter	correct	honor
body	cost	honorary
borrow	costs	hospital
borrowers	cottage	hot
bronze	crop	incorrect
catalog	dog	involved
clock	dollar	job
collar	drop	jobber
colleague	follow	knock
collect	followed	knowledge
college	foreign	lobby
co-op	golf	lock
cooperate	gone	locker
cooperative	holiday	logs

lot

model

moderate

modest

nobody

obligate

observe

occupancy

occupied

occur

occurrence

off

offer

office

officers

offset

often

on

operate

opposed

opposite

orange

origin

pocket

policy

polish

politics

popular

positive

problem

profit

project

promise

proper

property

prospect

prospective

rayon

remodeling

rob

rock

roster

shop

solid

solve

sorrow

sponsor

spot

stock

stop

top

topic

wash

watch

yacht

■ **AW**

abroad

across

all

author

authoritative

authorize

auto

ball

baseball

bought

broad

broadcasting

there will be · · · there would be · · · to their ·

They

as they	that they will	they have
as they are	they are	they may
before they	they are not	they may be
if they	they can	they will
if they are	they can be	they will be
if they are not	they can have	they will have
if they can	they cannot	they will not
if they would	they can't	they will see
if they would be	they did	they would
that they	they do	they would not
that they are	they do not	they would not be

This

as this	if this is the	this is
at this	in this	this is not
before this	in this case	this is the
by this	in this matter	this man
do this	of this	this matter
for this	on this	this may
hope that this	since this	this may be
if this	that this	this means
if this is	that this is	this will
if this is not	this can be	this would

this would be ⟋⟋   to this ⟋⟋   with this 𝒷

Which

in which 〳	on which the ⟍	which means ⟍ₒ𝒸
in which the 〵	which is 𝒥	which you 𝒽
in which you 〵	which is the ⟋	which you can 𝒽
of which 〳	which may ⟍ₒ	which you may 𝒽ₒ
on which 〵	which may be ⟍ₑ	with which 𝒪𝒥

Would

as you would 𝒬⟋	if you would 𝒬⟋	who would have ⟍⟋
as you would be 𝒬⟋	if you would be 𝒬⟋	who would not ⟍⟋
he would 𝒹	if you would have 𝒬⟋	would have ⟋
he would have 𝒹⟋	that would ⟍𝒹	you would ⟋
I would 𝒹	that would be ⟍𝒹⟋	you would be ⟋
I would have 𝒹⟋	who would ⟍	you would have ⟋
I would not 𝒹	who would be ⟍⟋	you would not ⟋

▪ WORD ENDING -LY

actively ⟋⟍	daily ⟋ₒ	favorably 𝒢
assembly 𝒬〳	deeply ⟍ₗ	firmly 𝒢⟍ₒ
badly 𝒢ₒ	duly ⟋ₒ	freely ⟨ₒ
barely 𝒷ₒ	earlier ℯℯ	greatly ⟍ₒₒ
briefly 𝒢	earliest ℯℓ	highly 𝒪
clearly ⟍ℯₒ	early ℯₒ	honestly ⟍ₑₒ
closely ⟍𝒳	earnestly ℯ⟍ₑₒ	inevitably 𝒻
costly 𝒴ₒ	fairly 𝒹ₒ	largely 𝒢⟍𝒢

lately ‿ℓ°   newly ‿ɔ   rarely ‿ℓ°

likely ‿ɔ°   nicely ‿ℓ   separately ℓ°

mainly ‿ɔ°   only ‿ɔ   sincerely ⱦℓ°

merely ‿ℓ°   positively ɛ   slightly ℓ°

mostly ‿ɣ°   possibly ℓ   strictly ℓ°

namely ‿ɔ°   precisely ℓ   surely ħℓ

nearly ‿ℓ°   presumably ℓ   thoroughly ℓℓ°

neatly ‿ℓ°   rapidly ℓ   truly ℓ°

lesson 9

▪ WORD ENDING -TION

action   declaration   installation

allocation   duplication   instruction

application   education   investigation

authorization   educational   irrigation

cancellation   election   legislation

caution   eradication   location

collection   fashion   mission

collision   inflation   motion

cooperation   insertion   national

corporation   inspection   nationally

correction   inspiration   nationwide

obligation	possession	protection
occasion	precaution	provision
occasionally	preparation	ration
occupation	prescription	relation
ocean	prevention	section
operation	profession	selection
option	professional	session
pension	promotion	solution
physician	promotional	supposition
pollution	proportion	television
portion	proportionate	vacation
position	proposition	vocational

■ WORD ENDINGS -CIENT, -CIENCY

| ancient | efficient | proficiency |
| efficiency | patient | proficient |

■ TO FOLLOWED BY A DOWNSTROKE

as to be	to bite	to check
has to be	to blame	to choose
is to be	to borrow	to face
to balance	to break	to fall
to be	to burn	to farm
to be sure	to buy	to feel
to bear	to change	to fill
to beat	to charge	to finance

to finish

to fit

to fly

to follow

to have

to have you

to park

to pass

to pay

to pick

to place

to plan

to play

to please

to post

to prepare

to preserve

to proceed

to produce

to promote

to protect

to protest

to prove

to provide

to say

to see

to select

to sell

to separate

to serve

to serve you

to share

to ship

to shoot

to show

to slide

to spare

to specify

to speed

to spread

to supply

to surprise

to survey

to verify

to visit

to which

to which the

to which you are

lesson 10

■ ND

assigned

band

behind

beyond

bind

binder

bindery

bond

bonded

brand

burned

calendar

candy

cleaned

cylinder

earned

end

fastened

find

friend

gained

grand

grind

happened

inclined

island

kind

kindest

land

learned

lend

lined

loaned

merchandise

mind

opened

owned

pending

phoned

planned

postponed

remainder

remained

remind

render

signed

spend

splendid

surrender

trained

trend

wind

wonder

wondering

▪ NT

absent

agent

apparent

applicant

aunt

bent

carpenter

cent

center

central

centralized

cogent

current

event

events

gentle

grant

granted

guarantee

haven't

hints

incentive

infants

inventory

isn't	printer	want
merchant	rent	wanted
paint	rental	warrant
parents	sent	warrants
plant	silent	went
planted	spent	winter
pleasant	talent	won't
plenty	urgent	
prevent	vacant	

■ ANT-, END-, ENT-, IND-, INT-

anticipate	entire	induce
anticipation	entirely	induced
antique	entry	intact
endorse	indicate	intelligence
endorsed	indication	intelligent
endorser	indicator	into

■ PHRASES

aren't	he didn't	I learned
as you will find	he finds	I sent
didn't	he isn't	if we don't
don't	I didn't	if you didn't
hadn't	I don't	if you don't
hasn't	I find	into it
haven't	I haven't	into that

into the	to prevent	who isn't
into these	to print	will find
into this	to spend	wouldn't
isn't	we can't	you aren't
isn't it	we wouldn't	you didn't
to bind	we find	you don't
to find	we don't	you haven't
to paint	we didn't	you will find
to plant	who didn't	you wouldn't

▪ SES

access	causes	insist
accessories	census	leases
addresses	chances	lenses
advances	classes	losses
advises	clauses	mattresses
analysis	closes	necessary
arises	courses	necessity
assessed	criticism	notices
assist	faces	nurses
balances	finances	offices
bases	glasses	passes
basis	horses	places
braces	increases	premises
cases	influences	presses

prices		proposes		sister	
process		reduces		sizes	
processes		releases		sources	
produces		says		spaces	
promises		services		versus	

lesson 11

■ BRIEF FORMS

after		and		from	
aftermath		hand		send	
afternoon		handle		should	
afterthought		handicap		street	
hereafter		handy		were	
thereafter		could		when	

■ PHRASES

After

after that		after them		after this	
after the		after these		after which	

And

and are		and his		and our	
and have		and is		and say	
and hope		and let		and see	

and that   ⟋○   and their   ⟋   and will   ⟋

and that is   ⟋ᵍ   and they   ⟋○   and will be   ⟋

and the   ⟋   and which   ⟋   and will not   ⟋

Could

could be   I could not   we could not

could not   I could see   we couldn't

could not be   I couldn't   who could

he could   if you could   you could

he could not   if we could   you could be

he couldn't   we could   you could have

I could   we could be   you could not

I could be   we could have   you could see

From

from him   from that   from this

from his   from the   from which

from it   from them   from you

from our   from these   hear from you

Send

send him   send this   sending the

send them   send you   sending you

Should

he should   I should   should be

he should be   I should have   should have

he should have   I should say   should not be

shouldn't | we should have | who should be

we should | we should say | you should

we should be | we shouldn't | you should be

we should see | who should | you should not

When

when our | when the | when they

when that | when these | when this

▪ RD

accordance | hardly | prepared

answered | hazard | record

appeared | heard | recorder

assured | hired | rendered

board | ignored | retired

border | incurred | stored

burden | inferred | surrendered

card | injured | tailored

cord | insured | third

favored | occurred | tired

garden | offered | toward

guard | pardon | ward

hard | postcard | wired

harder | preferred | word

▪ LD

billed | build | builders

called	folded	old
canceled	folder	oldest
child	gold	policyholder
children	golden	rolled
cold	handled	sealed
drilled	hauled	settled
entitled	held	shareholder
failed	holders	shoulder
field	holds	skilled
filed	installed	sold
filled	mailed	stockholder
fold	mild	told

▪ PHRASES

Rd

to board	to burden	to pardon

Ld

has called	I called	to build
he called	I sold	we failed
he sold	I told	we filled
he told	I traveled	we mailed

Been in Phrases

could have been	has been	have not been
had been	has not been	having been
had not been	have been	I have been

it has been   there have been   which have been

might have been   to have been   would have been

should have been   we have been   you have been

there has been   we have not been   you have not been

Able in Phrases

be able   he will be able   we may be able

been able   he will not be able   we might be able

being able   he would be able   we would not be able

has been able   I have not been able   will be able

has not been able   I will be able   you may be able

have not been able   to be able   you should be able

he may be able   we have been able   you will be able

he should be able   we have not been able   you would be able

chapter 3
lesson 13

■ BRIEF FORMS

circular 𝟨	order ✓	thanks ⌐
circulars 𝟨	ordered ✓	was 𝟀
enclose ⌐	orderly ✓	work ⌣
enclosed ⌐✓	soon 𝟤	worked ⌣✓
enclosure ⌐𝟤	sooner 𝟤⌣	worker ⌣⌐
glad ⌣	thank ⌐	workers ⌣⌐
gladly ⌣	thanked ⌐	yesterday 𝟫

■ PHRASES

Enclose

he enclosed ✓	I enclose ✓	we enclose ✓

Glad

be glad ⌣	I am glad ⌣	will be glad 𝟥
he will be glad 𝟥	they will be glad 𝟥	we will be glad 𝟥
he would be glad 𝟥	we would be glad 𝟥	I will be glad 𝟥

Order

in order ✓	in order that ✓	in order that the ✓

Thank

thank you ⌐	thank you for the 𝟤	thank you for your 𝟥
thank you for 𝟥	thank you for this 𝟥	to thank you for 𝟥

44

we thank you for ∂⟩   we thank you for the ∂⟩   we thank you for your ∂⟩

Was

and was	that it was	was it
he was	that there was	was made
I was	there was	was that
it was	this was	was the
it was the	this was the	which was

∎ U

above	cover	gulf
adjust	coverage	hundreds
adjuster	covered	hunting
ambitious	cup	husband
annum	cut	illustrate
blood	does	illustration
bonus	dozen	industry
bud	drug	just
bulbs	druggist	justice
bulk	duck	justify
bus	dug	justly
butter	dust	love
chorus	enormous	luck
color	enough	must
colored	famous	nervous
couple	generous	none

number	reduction	tough
numbered	religious	truck
numerous	rough	trust
nut	rub	unable
oven	rubber	uneven
plug	rust	up
plus	status	upon
product	succeed	us
production	suffer	utmost
productive	sufficient	utterly
prosperous	surplus	walnut
recover	thus	

▪ OO

book	full	put
booked	fulfill	stood
bookkeeping	handbook	sugar
booklet	look	took
bushel	looked	wood
cook	pull	woods
foot	pulled	wool
football	push	woolen

▪ PHRASES

Does

does not	does not have	doesn't

he does	that does not	who doesn't
he does not	this does not	which does

Must

he must	I must have	we must
he must be	must be	you must
he must have	must have	you must be
I must	that must be	you must be able
I must be	they must	you must have

Us

before us	gave us	send us
by us	give us	sending us
for us	giving us	to give us
from us	on us	with us

Miscellaneous

above the	I took	to push
he looks	I trust	to put
he took	to book	to trust
I look	to cover	we took
I looked	to cut	we trust

lesson 14

■ THE SOUND OF W IN THE BODY OF A WORD

acquaintance   acquainted   adequate

always

between

Broadway

dwelling

equip

equity

hardware

inadequate

liquid

meanwhile

qualify

queen

query

quick

quicker

quickest

quit

quite

quota

quote

railway

requisition

roadway

square

squarely

twice

twin

▪ TED

accepted

acted

adapted

adjusted

admitted

adopted

affected

asserted

attested

benefited

coasted

collected

cooperated

corrected

dated

duplicated

enumerated

fitted

hesitated

homestead

illustrated

incorporated

indicated

inserted

insisted

instead

instructed

invested

invited

lifted

limited

liquidated

listed

located

marketed

neglected

noted

omitted

operated

pasted

posted

protected

quoted  routed suited

rated selected tested

related separated treated

remitted solicited visited

rested started waited

rotated steady wasted

■ OTHERS

studied study today

■ DED

added deducted headed

dead deduction included

dedicated deducts loaded

dedication graded needed

deduct guided provided

■ OTHERS

audit credited ditto

auditor debt editor

candidate debtor editorial

candidates detail indebted

credit detailed indebtedness

■ PHRASES

he listed I needed I treated

he needed I noted we quoted

lesson 15

■ BRIEF FORMS

about		businesslike		thing	
any		doctor		things	
anybody		doctorate		think	
anyone		doctors		thinks	
anything		nothing		value	
business		once		valued	
businessman		one		what	
businesses		than		won	

■ PHRASES

About

about it		about that		about this	
about its		about the		about which	
about Mr.		about them		about you	
about my		about these		about your	

One

any one		one thing		only one	
each one		one-half		this one	
for one		one way		which one	

Than

less than		less than the	than the

50

Thing, Think

as you think	if they think	to think
do you think	if you think	we do not think
I do not think	same thing	who think
I think	they think	you think

What

| what are | what is | what will |
| what has been | what is the | what will be |

■ WORD ENDING -BLE

acceptable	capable	incapable
adaptable	deductible	liable
adjustable	double	payable
advisable	doubled	possible
agreeable	durable	profitable
applicable	eligible	reliable
appreciable	equitable	suitable
assembled	favorable	trouble
available	feasible	valuable
cable	honorable	visible

■ WORD BEGINNING RE-

reaction	reasonably	recent
reappear	rebate	reception
reason	receipt	rechecked
reasonable	receive	recipient

reciprocate	repaired	resolution
refer	repeat	resolve
reference	repeated	resources
referred	replace	respect
refining	replied	respond
reflect	reprint	response
reflected	reproduction	restrict
region	resale	resume
register	research	reveal
registration	reservation	revenue
rejected	reserve	reverse
reorder	reservoir	revise
repair	resist	revision

lesson 16

■ OI

annoyance	boy	invoice
annoyed	choice	invoices
appointed	coil	join
avoid	coin	joined
boiled	corduroy	joint
boiler	hoist	joy

lawyer ___ point ___ soiled ___

loyal ___ poison ___ spoiled ___

noise ___ royal ___ toy ___

oil ___ soil ___ voice ___

▪ PHRASES

to boil ___ to join ___ to point ___

▪ MAN

manage ___ mandatory ___ mansion ___

manager ___ manner ___ woman ___

▪ MEN

amend ___ many ___ mention ___

amended ___ meant ___ mentioned ___

businessmen ___ men ___ salesmen ___

cement ___ mental ___ tremendous ___

immensely ___ mentally ___ women ___

▪ MIN

administer ___ minimum ___ nominate ___

administrative ___ minimize ___ preliminary ___

aluminum ___ minister ___ prominence ___

eliminate ___ minute ___ prominent ___

mineral ___ nominal ___ seminar ___

▪ MON

harmonize ___ lemon ___ month ___

harmony ___ money ___ monthly ___

▪ PHRASES

as many	in this manner	this month
each month	in this month's	to mention
he mentioned	so many	we mention
I mention	these men	you mentioned

▪ YA, YE

yard	yearn	yellow
yarn	years	yes
yarns	yeast	yet
year	yell	yield

▪ PHRASES

Yet

as yet	has not yet been	I have not yet
has not yet	have not yet	is not yet

lesson 17

▪ BRIEF FORMS

accompanied	gentlemen	manufacturer
companies	importance	morning
company	important	next
elsewhere	manufacture	nowhere
gentleman	manufactured	short

shortage · shorthanded · whereabouts

shorter · shortly · whereas

shorthand · where · wherein

▪ PHRASES

this morning · we manufacture

Next

next month · next morning · next year

▪ WORD BEGINNING PER-

per · permanent · personally

percentage · permit · personnel

perfect · permitted · persuade

perfectly · person · persuaded

perhaps · personal · persuasion

▪ WORD BEGINNING PUR-

purchase · purple · pursue

purchased · purpose · pursued

purchases · pursuant · pursuit

▪ PHRASES

per hour · to permit · to purchase

per month · to persuade · to pursue

▪ WORD BEGINNING DE-

debit · decision · delegate

decide · delay · deliberate

decided · delayed · delighted

deliver	deposit	designed
delivered	deposited	designer
deliveries	depositor	designs
depend	depot	desirable
dependable	derive	desire
depended	deserve	desired
dependent	design	independence
depleted	designate	independent

■ WORD BEGINNING DI-

| diligently | directed | director |
| direct | direction | directory |

■ PHRASES

he decided	I desire	we decided
he desires	if you decide	we desire
I decided	if you desire	who desire

chapter 4
lesson 19

■ **BRIEF FORMS**

advertise	part	present
departing	participant	presentation
immediate	participate	presented
immediately	parties	represent
Ms.	partner	representative
opportunity	party	represented

■ **PHRASES**

on our part	to part	to present

■ **U**

accuse	huge	tube
acute	human	unanimous
argue	peculiar	unique
beautify	prosecute	unit
bureau	pure	unite
cubic	refusal	united
cure	refused	universal
few	refuses	use
fewer	review	used
fuel	tribune	uses

57

utilization   view   youth

▪ PHRASES

few days   few minutes   few months

▪ WORD ENDING -MENT

adjustment	document	momentary
advancement	elementary	movement
advertisement	elements	nonpayment
agreement	endorsement	payment
allotment	equipment	placement
amendment	establishment	replacement
apartment	garment	retirement
appointment	inducement	settlement
arrangement	installment	shipment
assessment	instrument	supplement
assignment	investment	supplementary
attachment	management	supplemented
basement	measurement	treatment
department	moment	

▪ PHRASES

few moments   in payment   to supplement

▪ WORD ENDING -TIAL (-CIAL)

beneficial	essentially	initial
especially	financial	initialed
essential	financially	official

partial   special   specialize

social   specialist   specialty

lesson 20

■ OW

account	boundary	foundry
accountant	brown	ground
accounted	clown	house
allow	council	household
allowance	counsel	houses
allowed	count	how
aloud	counted	loud
amount	counter	manpower
amounted	county	mounted
announce	cow	mouth
announced	crowded	now
announcement	doubt	ounce
announces	doubted	plow
around	down	pound
background	flour	powder
blouse	flowers	power
bound	found	proud

round    southeast   town

sound   surround   voucher

south   thousands   warehouse

▪ PHRASES

he found   I found   we count

I doubt   in our power   we doubt

I doubted   to count   we found

▪ WORD ENDING -THER

another   father   other

bother   feather   others

bothered   gather   otherwise

brother   gathered   rather

brotherly   leather   together

either   mother   weather

farther   neither   whether

▪ PHRASES

any other   I gathered   to bother

each other   many other   to gather

he gathered   other than

▪ WORD BEGINNING CON-

concealed   concern   concession

concentrate   concerned   conclude

conception   concert   concluded

conclusion ⌇

connected ⌇

contact ⌇

conclusive ⌇

connection ⌇

contest ⌇

concrete ⌇

conscientious ⌇

contract ⌇

conduct ⌇

consent ⌇

contracted ⌇

conducted ⌇

conservative ⌇

contractor ⌇

conductor ⌇

consider ⌇

contrary ⌇

confer ⌇

considerably ⌇

contrast ⌇

conference ⌇

consideration ⌇

control ⌇

confess ⌇

considered ⌇

controversy ⌇

confine ⌇

consign ⌇

convention ⌇

confinement ⌇

consigned ⌇

conversation ⌇

confined ⌇

consignment ⌇

conversion ⌇

confirm ⌇

consist ⌇

convert ⌇

confiscate ⌇

consisted ⌇

converted ⌇

confiscation ⌇

consolidate ⌇

convey ⌇

conflict ⌇

construct ⌇

conviction ⌇

confuse ⌇

constructed ⌇

convince ⌇

confused ⌇

construction ⌇

economic ⌇

confusion ⌇

constructive ⌇

economy ⌇

congested ⌇

consume ⌇

reconcile ⌇

congestion ⌇

consumer ⌇

reconstruction ⌇

▪ WORD BEGINNING COM-

accommodate ⌇

accomplishment ⌇

comedies ⌇

accomplish ⌇

combine ⌇

command ⌇

commence · commend · comment · commerce · commercial · commitments · committed · committee · commodities · commodity · common · commonly · compact · comparable · comparative

compare · compared · compel · compelled · compensate · compensation · compete · competitive · competitor · competitors · compiled · complaint · complete · completed · completion

compliment · complimentary · comply · composed · composer · composition · compound · comprehensive · compute · computer · incomprehensible · recommend · recommended

▪ PHRASES

he considered · to complete · to conserve

he considers · to comply · to consider

I consider · to conceal · to consist

if you consider · to confide · to convince

to compare · to confirm · we consider

to complain · to confuse · we considered

lesson 21

▪ BRIEF FORMS

advantage	everywhere	suggested
advantages	out	suggestion
ever	outlet	very
every	outline	whatever
everybody	outside	whenever
everyone	several	wherever
everything	suggest	without

▪ PHRASES

Ever, Every

ever since	every minute	every one
every day	every month	every other

Several

several days	several months	several others
several minutes	several other	

▪ DEN

accident	confidential	evident
condense	dental	evidently
condensed	deny	identify
confidence	evidence	incident
confident	evidenced	incidental

incidentally   residence   student

precedent   resident   sudden

president   residential   wooden

▪ OTHERS

abandon   danger   dinner

abandonment   dangerous   guidance

audience   dangerously   ingredients

▪ TEN

attend   intended   straighten

attendance   intention   straightened

attended   lieutenant   tenant

attention   maintenance   tend

attentive   patent   tendency

competent   pertinent   tender

consistent   potential   tendered

consistently   retention   tenderness

content   rotten   tennis

contention   sentence   tentative

intend   shorten   written

▪ TAN

acceptance   hesitancy   outstanding

assistance   inheritance   remittance

assistant   instance   resistance

constant   instant   stand

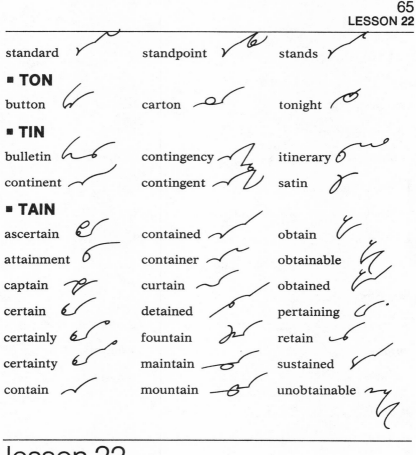

standard   standpoint   stands

■ **TON**

button   carton   tonight

■ **TIN**

bulletin   contingency   itinerary

continent   contingent   satin

■ **TAIN**

ascertain   contained   obtain

attainment   container   obtainable

captain   curtain   obtained

certain   detained   pertaining

certainly   fountain   retain

certainty   maintain   sustained

contain   mountain   unobtainable

lesson 22

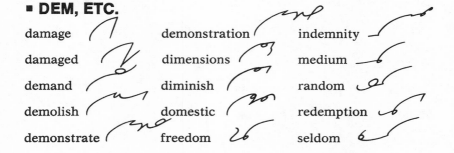

■ **DEM, ETC.**

damage   demonstration   indemnity

damaged   dimensions   medium

demand   diminish   random

demolish   domestic   redemption

demonstrate   freedom   seldom

■ TEM

attempt	item	systematic
attempted	items	temper
contemplate	itemized	temple
contemplated	system	temporary

■ TIM

estimate	intimated	optimistic
estimated	intimidate	testimony
intimate	legitimate	timber

■ TOM

accustomed	bottom	customer
automatic	custom	stomach
automobile	customary	tomorrow

■ SPECIAL BUSINESS PHRASES

to know	Dear Mr.	Cordially yours
to make	Dear Mrs.	Very sincerely yours
to me	My dear Miss	Very truly yours
Dear Ms.	My dear Mr.	Yours sincerely
Dear Miss	My dear Mrs.	Yours very sincerely

■ DAYS

Sunday	Wednesday	Saturday
Monday	Thursday	
Tuesday	Friday	

▪ MONTHS

January	May	September
February	June	October
March	July	November
April	August	December

▪ PHRASES

Friday morning	Saturday morning	Wednesday morning
Friday night	Tuesday morning	Thursday morning

lesson 23

▪ BRIEF FORMS

acknowledge	organize	overseas
acknowledged	organizer	oversight
acknowledgment	over	overwhelming
general	overcharge	question
generally	overdue	questionable
meantime	overhead	time
organization	overlooked	timer

▪ PHRASES

Time

about that time	about this time	at that time
about the time	any time	at the time

at this time	few times	one time
at which time	from time	several times
by that time	in time	since that time
by the time	many times	that time
by this time	of time	this time
each time	on time	to time

▪ DEF, DIF

defect	deferred	differ
defective	defined	difference
defense	definite	different
defer	defy	modify

▪ DEV, DIV

develop	devised	diverted
developed	devote	divide
development	devoted	divided
developer	diversified	dividend
device	diversion	division
devise	divert	divorce

▪ THE DOTTED CIRCLE

appreciate	appropriation	association
appreciated	area	aviation
appreciation	areas	bacteria
appreciative	associate	beneficiary
appropriate	associated	brilliant

comedian	initiative	obviate
create	librarian	piano
created	media	radiation
creative	negotiate	radiator
depreciation	negotiations	recreation
initiate	nuclear	variation

chapter 5
lesson 25

■ BRIEF FORMS

difficult	↗	requested	↗	success	↗
difficulty	↗	satisfaction	↗	under	↗
envelope	↗	satisfactorily	↗	understand	↗
estate	↗	satisfactory	↗	understandable	↗
progress	↗	satisfy	↗	understood	↗
progressive	↗	state	↗	undertake	↗
reinstate	↗	stated	↗	wish	↗
request	↗	statement	↗	wished	↗

■ WORDS MODIFIED IN PHRASES

As soon as

as soon as ↗   as soon as possible ↗   as soon as the ↗

I hope

I hope	↗	I hope the ↗	I hope to be ↗
I hope that	↗	I hope these ↗	I hope to see ↗
I hope that the ↗	I hope this ↗	I hope to have ↗

Let us

let us	↗	let us know ↗	let us say ↗
let us have	↗	let us make ↗	let us see ↗

70

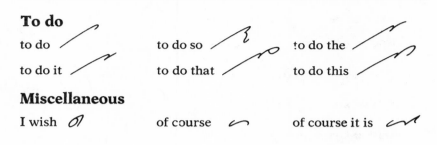

To do

to do

to do it

to do so

to do that

to do the

to do this

Miscellaneous

I wish

of course

of course it is

lesson 26

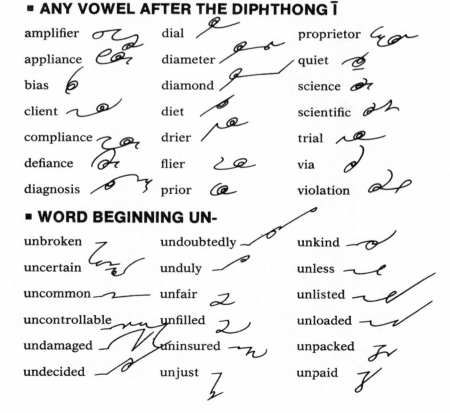

- **ANY VOWEL AFTER THE DIPHTHONG Ī**

amplifier

appliance

bias

client

compliance

defiance

diagnosis

dial

diameter

diamond

diet

drier

flier

prior

proprietor

quiet

science

scientific

trial

via

violation

- **WORD BEGINNING UN-**

unbroken

uncertain

uncommon

uncontrollable

undamaged

undecided

undoubtedly

unduly

unfair

unfilled

uninsured

unjust

unkind

unless

unlisted

unloaded

unpacked

unpaid

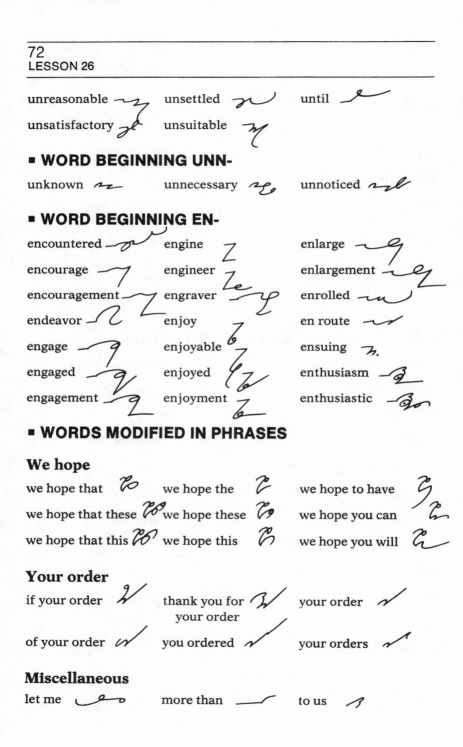

unreasonable   unsettled   until

unsatisfactory   unsuitable

▪ WORD BEGINNING UNN-

unknown   unnecessary   unnoticed

▪ WORD BEGINNING EN-

encountered   engine   enlarge

encourage   engineer   enlargement

encouragement   engraver   enrolled

endeavor   enjoy   en route

engage   enjoyable   ensuing

engaged   enjoyed   enthusiasm

engagement   enjoyment   enthusiastic

▪ WORDS MODIFIED IN PHRASES

We hope

we hope that   we hope the   we hope to have

we hope that these   we hope these   we hope you can

we hope that this   we hope this   we hope you will

Your order

if your order   thank you for your order   your order

of your order   you ordered   your orders

Miscellaneous

let me   more than   to us

lesson 27

▪ BRIEF FORMS

idea	particulars	regular
ideas	probable	regularly
newspaper	probably	speak
opinion	regard	speaker
particular	regarded	subject
particularly	regardless	subjected

▪ NG

along	length	strength
angle	linger	string
belong	long	strong
bring	longer	strongly
hanger	ring	swing
hung	sing	wrong
king	single	young
kingdom	song	youngster
language	spring	

▪ PHRASES

along the	as long	so long
along this	long time	

▪ NGK

anchor	ankle	anxious

73

bank 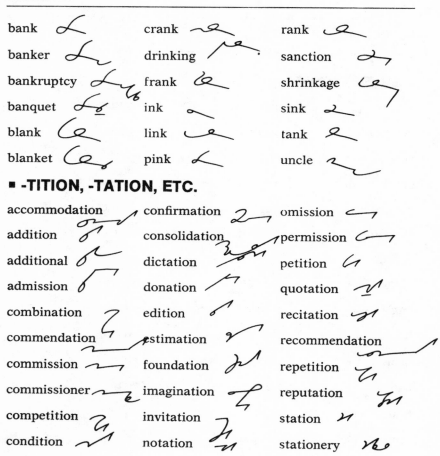	crank	rank
banker	drinking	sanction
bankruptcy	frank	shrinkage
banquet	ink	sink
blank	link	tank
blanket	pink	uncle

■ -TITION, -TATION, ETC.

accommodation	confirmation	omission
addition	consolidation	permission
additional	dictation	petition
admission	donation	quotation
combination	edition	recitation
commendation	estimation	recommendation
commission	foundation	repetition
commissioner	imagination	reputation
competition	invitation	station
condition	notation	stationery

lesson 28

■ AH, AW

ahead	awaited	award
await	awake	awarded

aware .✐   away .∂   awoke .↲

▪ X

affix ૨   flax ↲e   tax ℓ

appendix ℓ↲   flexible ↲ℓ   taxation ℓℓ

approximate ↳↲   index ↲↲   taxes ↳

box ↳   indexes ↲↲   taxicab ℓℓↄ

boxed ↳   maximum ↲e↲   taxpayer ℰↄ

boxes ↳   mix ↲e   text ℓe

fix ૨   mixer ↲e   textbook ℓↄ

fixes ↲   perplexing ℰℓ   wax ∂↲

▪ OMISSION OF SHORT U

Before n

apron ℓ   fun ↳   refund ↳↲

begun ↳↳   fund ↳   run ↲

blunder ↳↲   fundamental ↳↲   runner ↲↲

bunch ↳   gallon ↲ℓ   second ↳↲

bundles ↲↲   gun ↲↲   secondary ↳↲ℓ

country ↲ℓ   lunch ↲↲   son ↳

done ⁄   luncheon ↲↲   sun ↳

front ↲↳   punch ↳   ton ⌐

Before m

album ℓ↲   bumper ↳↲   consumption ↳↲

assumption ↲↳   column ↲ℓ   crumble ↲↲

become ↳↳   come ↲ℓ   crumple ↲↲

drum   presumption   somewhere

handsome   resumption   sum

income   some   summary

lumber   somebody   summer

lump   something   summons

overcome   sometime   vacuum

plumbing   sometimes   welcome

Before a Straight Downstroke

among   drunk   rush

brush   flush   rushed

brushed   functions   rushing

budget   judge   such

clutch   judgment   tongue

conjunction   junction   touch

crushed   much   trunk

■ PHRASES

among the   can't be done   must be done

among them   could be done   should be done

among these   has come   so much

as much   has done   some time

be done   have done   they come

being done   how much   to be done

can be done   I come   to become

cannot be done   I have done   to come

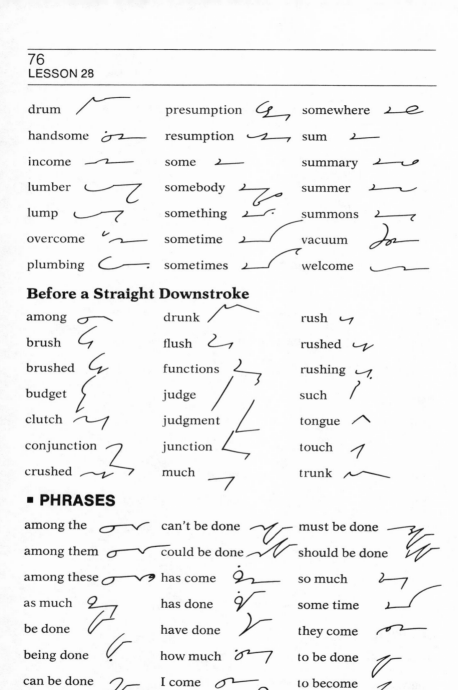

to judge 〰 who comes 〰 would be done 〰
too much 〰 who have done 〰
we have done 〰 will be done 〰

lesson 29

■ BRIEF FORMS

experience 〰 publish 〰 usual 〰
experienced 〰 published 〰 usually 〰
inexperienced 〰 publishers 〰 world 〰
ordinarily 〰 recognition 〰 worldly 〰
ordinary 〰 recognize 〰 worth 〰
public 〰 responsible 〰 worthless 〰
publication 〰 unusually 〰 worthy 〰

■ WORD BEGINNING EX-

exact 〰 except 〰 exclusive 〰
examination 〰 exception 〰 excuse 〰
examine 〰 exceptionally 〰 excuses 〰
examined 〰 excess 〰 executed 〰
examiner 〰 excessive 〰 exemption 〰
example 〰 exchange 〰 exhaust 〰
exceed 〰 excited 〰 exhausted 〰
excellent 〰 exclude 〰 exhibit 〰

exhibited	expensive	expressed
exhibition	experiment	expression
exist	experimental	extend
existed	expert	extended
existence	expiration	extension
expand	expire	extensive
expansion	expired	extensively
expect	explain	extent
expected	explained	exterior
expedite	explanation	extra
expend	explanatory	extraordinary
expended	explore	extreme
expense	exposition	extremely
expenses	express	inexpensive

▪ WORD ENDING -FUL

awful	grateful	powerful
beautiful	gratefully	respectfully
careful	helpful	successful
carefully	helpfulness	thoughtful
delightful	hopeful	useful
doubtful	hopefully	usefulness
faithful	meaningful	wonderful

▪ WORD ENDINGS -CAL, -CLE

analytical   article   automatically

basically	identically	political
chemical	logical	practical
clinical	logically	radical
critical	mechanical	surgical
economical	mechanically	technical
economically	medical	typical
historical	particle	vehicle
identical	physical	verticle

chapter 6
lesson 31

■ BRIEF FORMS

character ~	executive ~	nevertheless ~
characters ~	executives ~	object ~
characteristic ~	govern ~	objection ~
correspond ~	governed ~	objective ~
corresponded ~	government ~	quantities ~
correspondence ~	governor ~	quantity ~
corresponds ~	never ~	throughout ~

■ WORD ENDING -URE

century ~	future ~	pasture ~
departure ~	lecture ~	picture ~
departures ~	literature ~	procedure ~
expenditure ~	mature ~	procure ~
failure ~	miniature ~	secure ~
feature ~	moisture ~	signature ~
featured ~	natural ~	structure ~
figure ~	naturally ~	temperature ~
fixture ~	nature ~	venture ~

■ WORD ENDING -UAL

actual ~	actually ~	annual ~

80

annually	gradual	schedule
equal	gradually	scheduled
equally	individual	semiannual
eventually	manual	textual
factual	perpetual	virtually

lesson 32

■ WORD ENDING -ILY

easily	heartily	readily
families	heavily	steadily
family	necessarily	temporarily

■ WORD BEGINNING AL-

almost	alter	altered
already	alterable	although
also	alterations	altogether

■ WORD BEGINNING DIS-

disabled	disclose	discretion
disappoint	discount	discrimination
disappointment	discounted	discuss
disastrous	discouraged	discussion
disbursed	discovered	dislike
discharge	discrepancy	dismiss

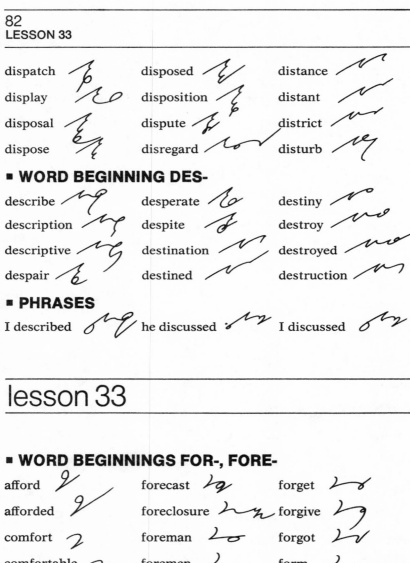

dispatch	disposed	distance
display	disposition	distant
disposal	dispute	district
dispose	disregard	disturb

■ WORD BEGINNING DES-

describe	desperate	destiny
description	despite	destroy
descriptive	destination	destroyed
despair	destined	destruction

■ PHRASES

I described   he discussed   I discussed

lesson 33

■ WORD BEGINNINGS FOR-, FORE-

afford	forecast	forget
afforded	foreclosure	forgive
comfort	foreman	forgot
comfortable	foremen	form
effort	foremost	formal
enforce	forerunner	former
enforcement	foresight	formula
force	forever	forth

forthcoming	inform	reinforce
fortunate	information	unfortunate
fortune	perform	uniform
fourth	performance	uniformly

■ WORD BEGINNING FUR-

furlough	furnish	further
furnace	furnished	furthermore
furnaces	furniture	furtive

■ PHRASES

inform us	setting forth	to forget
inform you	to force	to form
informing us	to forego	to furnish
set forth	to forfeit	to perform

■ AGO IN PHRASES

centuries ago	long ago	some time ago
days ago	months ago	some years ago
few days ago	several days ago	weeks ago
few months ago	several months ago	years ago

lesson 34

■ WANT IN PHRASES

he wanted	he wants	I want

I wanted	we want	who wanted
if you want	we wanted	you want
they want	who want	you wanted

■ ORT

airport	headquarters	quarterly
assort	mortal	report
assorted	port	reported
assortment	portable	reports
court	portfolio	resort
deportment	purport	sort
export	quart	sport
exportation	quarter	support

■ OMISSION OF R

alternate	eternal	southern
alternately	external	term
alternative	fraternity	terminal
attorney	modern	terminate
determination	northern	thermometer
determine	pattern	turn
determined	return	turned
eastern	returned	western

■ PHRASES

he returns	he turned	I returned

I turned   in return   to turn

- **MD, MT**

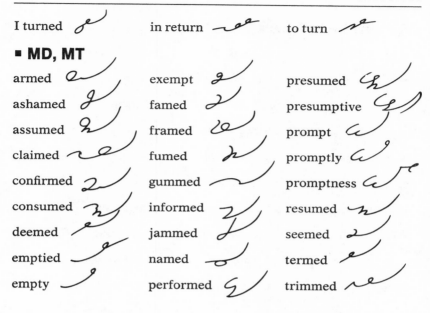

armed	exempt	presumed
ashamed	famed	presumptive
assumed	framed	prompt
claimed	fumed	promptly
confirmed	gummed	promptness
consumed	informed	resumed
deemed	jammed	seemed
emptied	named	termed
empty	performed	trimmed

lesson 35

- **WORD BEGINNING INTER-**

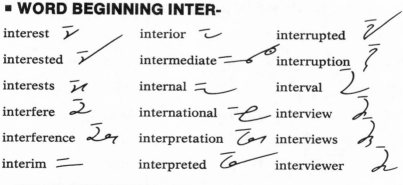

interest	interior	interrupted
interested	intermediate	interruption
interests	internal	interval
interfere	international	interview
interference	interpretation	interviews
interim	interpreted	interviewer

- **WORD BEGINNING INTR-**

introduce   introduced   introduction

■ WORD BEGINNINGS ENTER-, ENTR-

enter	entertain	entrance
entered	entertainer	entrances
enterprise	entertainment	unenterprising

■ WORD ENDING -INGS

bearings	feelings	meetings
beginnings	findings	offerings
buildings	furnishings	openings
casings	greetings	paintings
clippings	hearings	pleadings
drawings	holdings	proceedings
earnings	linings	savings
evenings	listings	servings

■ PHRASES

Friday mornings   in this morning's   this morning's

■ WORDS OMITTED IN PHRASES

at a loss	for a minute	in a few months
at a time	for a moment	in a position
bill of sale	glad to have	in addition to the
by the way	glad to know	in addition to this
day or two	glad to say	in order to be
for a few days	glad to see	in order to become
for a few minutes	I am of the opinion	in relation to the
for a long time	in a few days	in the future

87
LESSON 35

in the past	one of the best	some of our
in the world	one of the most	some of the
line of business	one of them	some of them
line of goods	one of these	some of these
many of the	one or two	some of this
many of them	ought to have	son-in-law
men and women	out of date	two or three
none of the	out of that	up and down
none of them	out of the	up to date
on the subject	out of the question	we are of the opinion
one of our	out of them	week or two
one of the	out of this	will you please

chapter 7
lesson 37

■ **WORD ENDING -INGLY**

accordingly · convincingly · increasingly

amazingly · entertainingly · seemingly

approvingly · exceedingly · willingly

■ **WORD BEGINNING IM-**

impact · imposed · imprinted

impairment · impossible · improper

impartial · impracticable · improved

imperative · impress · improvement

implements · impression · reimburse

import · imprint · reimbursement

■ **WORD BEGINNING IMM-**

immaterial · immodest · immoderate

■ **WORD BEGINNING EM-**

embarrass · emphasis · employed

embarrassment · emphasize · employees

emblem · emphatically · employment

embraces · empire · unemployed

■ **OMISSION OF MINOR VOWEL**

auditorium · companion · courteous

curious	millions	serious
erroneous	obvious	situation
evaluate	period	situated
evaluation	periodical	theory
genuine	periodically	undergraduate
graduate	previous	union
graduation	previously	valuation
ideal	radius	various
junior	senior	volume

lesson 38

■ WORD ENDING -SHIP

authorship	kinship	relationship
fellowship	leadership	scholarship
flagship	membership	steamship
friendship	ownership	township
hardship	partnership	workmanship

■ WORD BEGINNING SUB-

subcommittee	sublet	subscribe
subdivision	submission	subscriber
subeditor	submit	subscription
subhead	subordinate	substance

substantial   substantiate   suburbs

substantially   subtracted   subway

■ WORD ENDING -ULATE

accumulate   circulated   regulate

accumulated   circulating   stimulate

calculate   congratulate   stimulated

calculator   formulate   stimulates

■ WORD ENDING -ULATION

accumulation   population   stimulation

circulation   regulation   stipulation

congratulations   speculation   tabulation

■ WORD ENDING -RITY

authorities   integrity   prosperity

charity   majority   securities

clarity   maturity   surety

lesson 39

■ WORD ENDING -LITY

ability   feasibility   locality

advisability   fidelity   nobility

disability   inability   personality

facility   liabilities   possibilities

qualities   responsibility   stability

reliability   sensibilities   utilities

▪ WORD ENDING -LTY

casualty   loyalty   royalties

faculty   penalty   royalty

▪ WORD ENDINGS -SELF, -SELVES

herself   myself   themselves

himself   oneself   yourself

itself   ourselves   yourselves

▪ PHRASES

for itself   for themselves   in itself

for myself   for yourself   of ourselves

for ourselves   for yourselves   with themselves

lesson 40

▪ ABBREVIATING PRINCIPLE

-Tribute, -Tribution

attribute   contribution   distribution

contribute   distribute   distributors

contributed   distributed   retribution

-Quent

consequently   delinquent   eloquent

frequent	frequently	subsequent

-Quire

acquire	esquire	inquiry
acquired	inquire	require
acquirement	inquiries	requirements

-Titute, -Titution

constitute	institute	substitute
constitution	institution	substitution

-Titude

aptitude	fortitude	latitude
attitude	gratitude	

-Ology

apologies	biology	psychology
apologize	physiology	technology
apology	psychological	terminology

-Itis

appendicitis	neuritis	tonsillitis

-Ntic

Atlantic	authentic	frantic

-Iety

propriety	society	variety

lesson 41

▪ ABBREVIATING PRINCIPLE -GRAPH

paragraph	telegraph	stenography
phonograph	stenographer	typographical
photograph	stenographic	typographically

▪ ABBREVIATING PRINCIPLE (Concluded)

algebra	equivalent	privilege
alphabet	inconvenience	privileged
alphabetical	inconvenienced	reluctance
anniversary	inconvenient	reluctant
arithmetic	mathematics	significance
convenience	memoranda	significant
convenient	memorandum	statistic
conveniently	philosophy	statistical

▪ WORD BEGINNING TRANS-

transact	transfers	transmit
transaction	transistor	transmitted
transcribe	transit	transparent
transcript	transition	transplant
transcription	translated	transport
transfer	translation	transportation
transferred	transmission	transposition

93

chapter 8
lesson 43

■ WORD BEGINNING MIS-

miscarry	mislaid	mistaken
miscellaneous	misleading	mistook
misconception	misplaced	misunderstanding
misfortune	misprint	misunderstood
misinformation	mistake	mystery

■ WORD BEGINNING SUPER-

superb	superintendent	supervision
superficially	superior	supervisor

■ OMISSION OF E FROM U

communicate	continue	monument
communicated	continued	municipal
communication	continues	music
communities	continuous	musical
community	discontinue	mutual
continuance	manuscript	mutually

94

lesson 44

■ WORD BEGINNING SELF-

self-addressed   self-defense   selfish

self-assurance   self-educated   self-made

self-contained   self-explanatory   self-reliance

self-confidence   self-improvement   self-satisfied

self-control   self-interest   self-supporting

■ WORD BEGINNING CIRCUM-

circumstance   circumstances   circumvent

■ WORD ENDING -IFICATION

certification   identification   qualifications

clarification   justification   ratification

classification   modification   specifications

gratification   notification   verification

lesson 45

■ WORD ENDING -HOOD

boyhood   hardihood   neighborhood

childhood   manhood   parenthood

■ WORD ENDING -WARD

afterward   awkward   backward

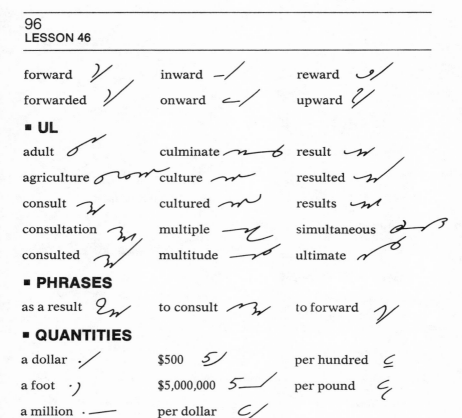

| forward | inward | reward |
| forwarded | onward | upward |

▪ UL

adult	culminate	result
agriculture	culture	resulted
consult	cultured	results
consultation	multiple	simultaneous
consulted	multitude	ultimate

▪ PHRASES

| as a result | to consult | to forward |

▪ QUANTITIES

a dollar	$500	per hundred
a foot	$5,000,000	per pound
a million	per dollar	

lesson 46

▪ WORD ENDING -GRAM

| cablegram | monogram | programmed |
| diagram | program | telegram |

▪ WORD BEGINNINGS ELECTRIC-, ELECTR-

| electric | electrically | electricity |
| electrical | electrician | electric wire |

electronics ⟋ electros ⟋ electrotype ⟋

■ COMPOUNDS

anyhow ⟋	notwithstanding ⟋	within ⟋
anywhere ⟋	someone ⟋	withstand ⟋
heretofore ⟋	thereupon ⟋	withstood ⟋
however ⟋	whereupon ⟋	worthwhile ⟋

■ INTERSECTION

Chamber of Commerce ⟋	c.o.d. ⟋	a.m. ⟋
vice versa ⟋	p.m. ⟋	

lesson 47

■ GEOGRAPHICAL TERMINATIONS -BURG

Fitchburg ⟋	Harrisburg ⟋	Pittsburgh ⟋
Greensburg ⟋	Newburgh ⟋	Plattsburg ⟋

■ -INGHAM

Buckingham ⟋	Cunningham ⟋	Framingham ⟋

■ -INGTON

Arlington ⟋	Huntington ⟋	Torrington ⟋
Bloomington ⟋	Irvington ⟋	Washington ⟋
Burlington ⟋	Lexington ⟋	Wilmington ⟋

▪ -VILLE

Brownsville	Coatesville	Evansville
Gainesville	Knoxville	Nashville
Jacksonville	Louisville	Zanesville

Appendix

frequently used words

The following list contains 500 frequently used words in alphabetical order along with their Gregg Shorthand outlines.

1. a
2. able
3. about
4. above
5. accept
6. accordance
7. account
8. acknowledge
9. action
10. additional
11. address
12. addressed
13. advance
14. advertising
15. advise
16. advised
17. after
18. again

19. against
20. ago
21. all
22. along
23. already
24. also
25. although
26. always
27. am
28. amount
29. an
30. and
31. another
32. answer
33. any
34. anything
35. appreciate
36. appreciated

37. approval
38. are
39. arrange
40. as
41. ask
42. asked
43. asking
44. assure
45. at
46. attached
47. attention
48. back
49. bad
50. balance
51. bank
52. basis
53. be
54. because

55. bed	79. card	103. connection
56. been	80. care	104. consider
57. before	81. careful	105. consideration
58. being	82. case	106. contract
59. believe	83. cases	107. convenience
60. best	84. cash	108. copies
61. better	85. catalogue	109. copy
62. between	86. certain	110. correct
63. big	87. certainly	111. correspondence
64. bill	88. change	112. cost
65. book	89. charge	113. could
66. books	90. charged	114. course
67. both	91. charges	115. cover
68. boy	92. check	116. covering
69. bring	93. city	117. credit
70. business	94. claim	118. customer
71. but	95. class	119. date
72. by	96. close	120. dated
73. call	97. collection	121. day
74. called	98. come	122. days
75. calling	99. coming	123. delay
76. can	100. company	124. delivery
77. cannot	101. complete	125. department
78. car	102. condition	126. desire

127. did
128. different
129. direct
130. discount
131. do
132. does
133. doing
134. done
135. doubt
136. dozen
137. draft
138. duplicate
139. during
140. each
141. earliest
142. early
143. either
144. enclose
145. enclosed
146. enclosing
147. enough
148. entire
149. entirely
150. error

151. every
152. expect
153. expense
154. express
155. fact
156. factory
157. far
158. favor
159. feel
160. few
161. file
162. find
163. first
164. following
165. for
166. form
167. forward
168. forwarded
169. found
170. freight
171. from
172. full
173. furnish
174. further

175. future
176. general
177. gentleman
178. get
179. getting
180. give
181. given
182. giving
183. glad
184. go
185. going
186. good
187. goods
188. got
189. great
190. greatly
191. had
192. hand
193. handle
194. handling
195. has
196. have
197. having
198. he

199. hear
200. help
201. her
202. here
203. herewith
204. high
205. him
206. his
207. hold
208. hope
209. house
210. how
211. however
212. I
213. if
214. immediate
215. in
216. indeed
217. information
218. inquiry
219. instructions
220. interest
221. interested
222. into

223. invoice
224. is
225. issue
226. it
227. item
228. items
229. its
230. just
231. keep
232. kind
233. kindly
234. know
235. large
236. last
237. later
238. less
239. let
240. letter
241. letters
242. like
243. line
244. list
245. little
246. long

247. look
248. lot
249. made
250. mail
251. make
252. making
253. man
254. many
255. material
256. matter
257. matters
258. may
259. me
260. meet
261. meeting
262. memorandum
263. men
264. merchandise
265. might
266. mind
267. money
268. month
269. months
270. more

271. morning
272. most
273. much
274. must
275. my
276. name
277. near
278. necessary
279. need
280. new
281. next
282. no
283. not
284. note
285. nothing
286. notice
287. now
288. number
289. oblige
290. of
291. off
292. offer
293. office
294. old

295. on
296. once
297. one
298. only
299. open
300. opportunity
301. or
302. order
303. ordered
304. orders
305. original
306. other
307. our
308. out
309. over
310. own
311. page
312. paid
313. paper
314. part
315. particular
316. past
317. pay
318. payment

319. people
320. personal
321. place
322. placed
323. please
324. pleased
325. pleasure
326. point
327. policy
328. position
329. possible
330. present
331. price
332. prices
333. probably
334. prompt
335. promptly
336. proper
337. purchase
338. put
339. question
340. quite
341. rate
342. rather

343. reach	367. requested	391. several
344. reason	368. return	392. shall
345. receipt	369. returned	393. she
346. receive	370. returning	394. ship
347. received	371. right	395. shipment
348. recent	372. sale	396. shipped
349. recently	373. sales	397. shipping
350. record	374. same	398. short
351. records	375. sample	399. should
352. refer	376. satisfactory	400. show
353. reference	377. saw	401. showing
354. referred	378. say	402. since
355. referring	379. school	403. sir
356. regard	380. second	404. size
357. regarding	381. secure	405. small
358. regret	382. see	406. so
359. regular	383. seems	407. sold
360. relative	384. sell	408. some
361. remain	385. send	409. something
362. remittance	386. sending	410. soon
363. reply	387. sent	411. sorry
364. replying	388. separate	412. special
365. report	389. service	413. state
366. request	390. settlement	414. stated

415. statement
416. still
417. stock
418. subject
419. such
420. suggest
421. supply
422. sure
423. take
424. taken
425. taking
426. than
427. thank
428. thanking
429. that
430. the
431. their
432. them
433. there
434. therefore
435. these
436. they
437. thing
438. think

439. this
440. three
441. through
442. time
443. to
444. today
445. together
446. too
447. total
448. trouble
449. truly
450. trust
451. trusting
452. try
453. two
454. unable
455. under
456. understand
457. unless
458. until
459. up
460. upon
461. us
462. use

463. used
464. value
465. very
466. want
467. was
468. way
469. we
470. week
471. weeks
472. well
473. were
474. what
475. when
476. whether
477. which
478. while
479. who
480. why
481. will
482. wire
483. wish
484. wishes
485. with
486. within

487. without

488. work

489. would

490. write

491. writer

492. writing

493. written

494. wrote

495. year

496. years

497. yet

498. you

499. your

500. yours

index to words

(Note: a, 3 means that the word may first be written in Lesson 3, in Gregg Shorthand, Series 90.)

designer, 17
designs, 17
desirable, 17
desire, 17
desired, 17
desk, 5
despair, 32
desperate, 32
despite, 32
destination, 32
destined, 32
destiny, 32
destroy, 32
destroyed, 32
destruction, 32
detail, 14
detailed, 14
detained, 21
determination, 34
determine, 34
determined, 34
develop, 23
developed, 23
developer, 23
development, 23
device, 23
devise, 23
devised, 23
devote, 23
devoted, 23
diagnosis, 26
diagram, 46
dial, 26
diameter, 26
diamond, 26
dictate, 5
dictation, 27
did, 5
diet, 26
differ, 23
difference, 23
different, 23
difficult, 25
difficulty, 25
dig, 5
diligently, 17
dimensions, 22
diminish, 22
dinner, 21
direct, 17
directed, 17
direction, 17
director, 17
directory, 17
disability, 39
disabled, 32
disappoint, 32
disappointment, 32
disastrous, 32
disbursed, 32
discharge, 32
disclose, 32
discontinue, 43
discount, 32
discounted, 32
discouraged, 32
discovered, 32
discrepancy, 32
discretion, 32

discrimination, 32
discuss, 32
discussion, 32
dishes, 7
dislike, 32
dismiss, 32
dispatch, 32
display, 32
disposal, 32
dispose, 32
disposed, 32
disposition, 32
dispute, 32
disregard, 32
distance, 32
distant, 32
distribute, 40
distributed, 40
distribution, 40
distributors, 40
district, 32
disturb, 32
ditto, 14
diversified, 23
diversion, 23
divert, 23
diverted, 23
divide, 23
divided, 23
dividend, 23
division, 23
divorce, 23
do, 4
doctor, 15
doctorate, 15
doctors, 15
document, 19
does, 13
dog, 7
dollar, 7
domestic, 22
donation, 27
done, 28
door, 2
double, 15
doubled, 15
doubt, 20
doubted, 20
doubtful, 29
down, 20
dozen, 13
draft, 5
drag, 5
drain, 2
dramatic, 5
drastic, 5
draw, 7
drawer, 7
drawings, 35
drawn, 7
drew, 4
drier, 26
drill, 5
drilled, 11
drinking, 27
drive, 2
driver, 2
drop, 7
drove, 2

drug, 13
druggist, 13
drum, 28
drunk, 28
dry, 2
duck, 13
due, 4
dug, 13
duly, 8
duplicate, 5
duplicated, 14
duplication, 9
durable, 15
during, 4
dust, 13
duty, 4
dwelling, 14
dye, 2

E
each, 7
eager, 4
earlier, 8
earliest, 8
early, 8
earn, 5
earned, 10
earnest, 5
earnestly, 8
earnings, 35
earth, 5
ease, 1
easiest, 2
easily, 32
east, 1
Easter, 2
eastern, 34
easy, 1
economic, 20
economical, 29
economically, 29
economy, 20
edges, 7
edition, 27
editor, 14
editorial, 14
education, 9
educational, 9
effect, 5
effective, 5
efficiency, 9
efficient, 9
effort, 33
either, 20
elastic, 5
elect, 5
election, 9
electric, 46
electric wire, 46
electrical, 46
electrically, 46
electrician, 46
electricity, 46
electronics, 46
electros, 46
electrotype, 46
elementary, 19
elements, 19
eligible, 15

eliminate, 16
eloquent, 40
else, 5
elsewhere, 17
embarrass, 37
embarrassment, 37
emblem, 37
embraces, 37
emphasis, 37
emphasize, 37
emphatically, 37
empire, 37
employed, 37
employees, 37
employment, 37
emptied, 34
empty, 34
enable, 5
enact, 5
enamel, 5
enclose, 13
enclosed, 13
enclosure, 13
encountered, 26
encourage, 26
encouragement, 26
end, 10
endeavor, 26
endorse, 10
endorsed, 10
endorsement, 19
endorser, 10
energy, 5
enforce, 33
enforcement, 33
engage, 26
engaged, 26
engagement, 26
engine, 26
engineer, 26
engraver, 26
enjoy, 26
enjoyable, 26
enjoyed, 26
enjoyment, 26
enlarge, 26
enlargement, 26
enormous, 13
enough, 13
enrolled, 26
en route, 26
ensuing, 26
enter, 35
entered, 35
enterprise, 35
entertain, 35
entertainer, 35
entertainingly, 37
entertainment, 35
enthusiasm, 26
enthusiastic, 26
entire, 10
entirely, 10
entitled, 11
entrance, 35
entrances, 35
entry, 10
enumerated, 14
envelope, 25

seminar, 16
senate, 5
senator, 5
send, 11
senior, 37
sense, 5
sensibilities, 39
sent, 10
sentence, 21
separate, 5
separated, 14
separately, 8
September, 22
series, 3
serious, 37
serve, 5
service, 5
services, 10
servings, 35
session, 9
set, 5
settle, 5
settled, 11
settlement, 19
several, 21
sew, 2
shade, 7
shall, 7
shape, 7
shaped, 7
shapes, 7
share, 7
shareholder, 11
sharp, 7
she, 7
sheets, 7
shelf, 7
shell, 7
shelves, 7
ship, 7
shipment, 19
shipped, 7
shoe, 7
shoes, 7
shoot, 7
shop, 7
short, 17
shortage, 17
shorter, 17
shorthand, 17
shorthanded, 17
shortly, 17
should, 11
shoulder, 11
show, 7
shown, 7
shows, 7
shrinkage, 27
sickness, 5
side, 2
sides, 3
siege, 7
sight, 2
sign, 2
signature, 31
signed, 10
significance, 41
significant, 41
silent, 10

silver, 5
similar, 5
simple, 5
simultaneous, 45
since, 5
sincere, 5
sincerely, 8
sing, 27
single, 27
sink, 27
sister, 10
situated, 37
situation, 37
sizes, 10
sketch, 7
skiing, 4
skilled, 11
slack, 5
slice, 3
slide, 3
slight, 3
slightly, 8
slowest, 5
small, 7
smaller, 7
smart, 5
smile, 2
smoke, 4
smooth, 5
snow, 2
so, 2
soap, 3
social, 19
society, 40
soft, 7
soil, 16
soiled, 16
sold, 11
solicit, 5
solicited, 14
solid, 7
solution, 9
solve, 7
some, 28
somebody, 28
someone, 46
something, 28
sometime, 28
sometimes, 28
somewhere, 28
son, 28
song, 27
soon, 13
sooner, 13
sorrow, 7
sort, 34
sound, 20
source, 3
sources, 10
south, 20
southeast, 20
southern, 34
space, 3
spaces, 10
spare, 3
speak, 27
speaker, 27
special, 19
specialist, 19

specialize, 19
specialty, 19
specific, 4
specifications, 44
specify, 5
speculation, 38
speech, 7
speed, 3
spend, 10
spent, 10
splendid, 10
spoiled, 16
spoke, 4
sponsor, 7
sport, 34
spot, 7
spread, 5
spring, 27
square, 14
squarely, 14
stability, 39
staff, 5
stain, 1
stamp, 5
stand, 21
standard, 21
standpoint, 21
stands, 21
star, 5
start, 5
started, 14
state, 25
stated, 25
statement, 25
station, 27
stationery, 27
statistic, 41
statistical, 41
status, 13
stay, 1
stayed, 1
steadily, 32
steady, 14
steam, 1
steamship, 38
stenographer, 41
stenographic, 41
stenography, 41
step, 5
stereo, 2
still, 1
stimulate, 38
stimulated, 38
stimulates, 38
stimulation, 38
stipulation, 38
stock, 7
stockholder, 11
stomach, 22
stone, 2
stood, 13
stop, 7
storage, 7
store, 2
stored, 11
storm, 2
story, 2
stove, 2
stow, 2

straighten, 21
straightened, 21
strategy, 7
stream, 2
street, 11
strength, 27
strictly, 8
strike, 4
string, 27
strive, 2
strong, 27
strongly, 27
structure, 31
student, 21
studied, 14
study, 14
style, 2
styles, 3
subcommittee, 38
subdivision, 38
subeditor, 38
subhead, 38
subject, 27
subjected, 27
sublet, 38
submission, 38
submit, 38
subordinate, 38
subscribe, 38
subscriber, 38
subscription, 38
subsequent, 40
substance, 38
substantial, 38
substantially, 38
substantiate, 38
substitute, 40
substitution, 40
subtracted, 38
suburbs, 38
subway, 38
succeed, 13
success, 25
successful, 29
such, 28
sudden, 21
suffer, 13
sufficient, 13
sugar, 13
suggest, 21
suggested, 21
suggestion, 21
suit, 4
suitable, 15
suited, 14
sum, 28
summary, 28
summer, 28
summons, 28
sun, 28
Sunday, 22
superb, 43
superficially, 43
superintendent, 43
superior, 43
supervision, 43
supervisor, 43
supplement, 19
supplementary, 19